A true story from the Bible

GOD'S VERY COLORFUL CREATION

·WRITTEN BY·
Tim Thornborough

·ILLUSTRATED BY·
Jennifer Davison

How many colors of the rainbow can you name? There are seven. But there are also many, many more colors in the rainbow, because there are so many different kinds of blue and green and yellow and red.

And each one has a different name — light blue, dark blue, middle blue and so on.

This is a book about how God made his very good and very wonderful world, with every shade of the rainbow, and so many more. As you read the words, try to point to the different colors on the page, and discover lots of different names of all the fantastic shades in God's very good and very wonderful world.

God's Very Colorful Creation © The Good Book Company, 2021, 2022 (twice).
Words by Tim Thornborough. Illustrations by Jennifer Davison. Design and art direction by André Parker.
thegoodbook.com • thegoodbook.co.uk • thegoodbook.com.au • thegoodbook.co.nz • thegoodbook.co.in
ISBN: 9781784986339. Printed in Turkey.

In the beginning, God created
the heavens and the earth.

Everything was dark but God's
Spirit was there, getting ready
to do something amazing.

And God said,
"Let there be..."

LiGHT!

The light was...

bright and blazing,
shiny and shimmering,
gleaming and glowing.

And the dark was...

dusky,

dim,

and deep.

And on the second
day God made the
sky and the sea.

The sky was
azure and cobalt,
periwinkle and powder blue,
baby blue and midnight blue.

And the sea was
teal and turquoise,
aquamarine and ultramarine,
and sometimes sea-green and gray.

And on the third day God
made the dry land appear.

It was brown and beige,
chestnut and chocolate,
tan and taupe.

And the mighty majestic mountains were
gray and granite and purple and puce,

with dots of gold and silver, ruby and emerald
and shimmering, sparkling diamond.

And God told the land to start sprouting plants, and it did.

Leaves that were green and yellow and gold and scarlet.

Flowers and fruit that
were orange and pink
and pumpkin and plum and
peach and papaya.

"This is good," said God.
"It is so, so good."

And on the fourth day
God made the sun shine with
gleaming golds and yellows.

And at night the
moon shone with a
cold gray light.

And God flung stars and
galaxies into space.

Red giants and white dwarfs.
Colorful swirling nebulas of
magenta, ocher, and violet.

"This is good," said God.
"It is so, so good."

And on the fifth day
God filled the sea with
fantastic creatures.

Goldfish and pink salmon.
Whitebait and yellowfin tuna.

And God made octopuses and cuttlefish that could change their color whenever they wanted to.

The sky came alive to the sound of flapping wings.

Blackbirds and bluebirds, goldcrest and greenfinch.

Dragonflies and butterflies,
and practically perfect peacocks.

And on the sixth day
God spoke and the animals appeared.

Brown bears and
black widow spiders.

Stripy zebras and
golden giraffes.

Red deer and
baboons with
pink bottoms
and every-color
chameleons.

"This is good," said God,
"It is so, so good.
But now it's time for
the best of all!"

"Let us make people in our own image," said God.

"And let them grow and fill the earth." And God made men and women to have beautiful and fabulous variety.

Their skins would be black and brown and tan and rosy pink.

Their hair would be red and blond and chestnut and raven black.

"Oh, this is good," said God. "It's so very, very good."

And God blessed his very colorful creation, which was...

red and
orange and
yellow and green and
blue and indigo and violet and
gold and every single color
you can imagine!

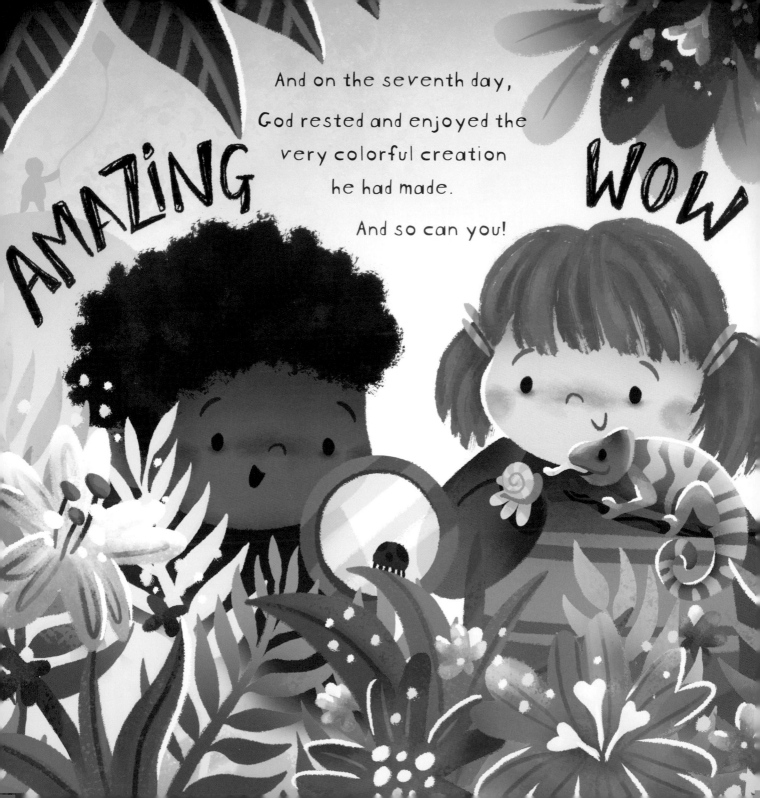

And on the seventh day,
God rested and enjoyed the
very colorful creation
he had made.
And so can you!

AMAZING

WOW